Learning Analytics in SQL for Beginners

Djoni Darmawikarta

Table of Contents

Introduction

Progressive organizations, both businesses and public services, around the world have adopted analytics. Thanks to the recent availability of **SQL analytic functions** they can now do their analytics right on the database.

You should jump on the bandwagon now!

If you want to learn SQL analytic functions, this is the book of choice.

It is a practical book, teaching you how to use the SQL analytic function step-by-step using examples.

When you finish the book, you'd be ready to apply your analytics skill in real-world projects.

Before we move on, I need to clarify a terminology. In some databases, including in SQLite, analytic function is called window function. As this book uses SQLite, I opt for **window function** instead of analytic function. So, from now on, in this book, I will use window function.

SQLite is an open source relational database, which you can download from:

Though the book examples use SQLite, very similar window functions are available in many other databases, including Oracle, MySQL and MS SQL Server. You can apply what you learn from this book on those other databases.

Prerequisite Skill

This book assumes that you are familiar with SQL. If you need to learn or refresh your SQL skill, you can read my book *Learning SQL in SQLite for Beginners*.

Book Examples

To learn the most out of this book, try the book examples. The number of rows of the table used in the examples is purposely small to facilitate your learning.

Software Requirements

I wrote and tested the book examples in **DB Browser for SQLite**, which is an open source GUI for specifically working with SQLite database. The SQL statement and its result are shown in this book as screenshots. So, in addition to SQLite, you will want to have an installation of DB Browser for SQLite , which you can download from https://sqlitebrowser.org/dl/

Appendix A briefly introduces DB Browser for SQLite. More specifically how to use it for creating a database, which you will use to try the book examples, inserting rows (especially NULL to a column), and of course querying.

If you want to you can type and execute the SQL statements of the book examples in the **SQLite command-line shell** window. The output will not be as visually friendly as that on the DB Browser for SQLite. SQLite command-line shell is a SQLite tool that you can also download from the SQLite web site. If you are curious about it, consult Appendix B: Command-line shell.

Chapter 1 Introducing Window Function

Aggregate function is no stranger to those who have been using SQL. So, how is window function different from aggregate function?

Aggregate function vs. Window function

They are the same in the sense that both aggregate and window functions operate on **multiple rows**.

But, the results of the queries where the function are used are different.

Let's use an example to further clarify.

We will use data in a **sales** table created by the following CREATE TABLE statement.

```
CREATE TABLE sales (
        year    INTEGER,
        month   INTEGER,
        month_name    TEXT,
        date    INTEGER,
        amount NUMERIC
);
```

When we add rows using the following statement …

```
INSERT INTO sales (year, month, month_name, date, amount)
VALUES ('2020', '1', 'JAN', '1', '10')
,('2020', '1', 'JAN', '1', '15')
,('2020', '2', 'FEB', '2', '20')
,('2020', '2', 'FEB', '6', '60')
,('2020', '3', 'MAR', '9', '90')
,('2020', '4', 'APR', '9', '95')
,('2020', '5', 'MAY', '10', '100')
,('2021', '2', 'FEB', '4', '40')
,('2021', '2', 'FEB', '5', '50')
```

```
,('2022', '2', 'FEB', '6', '60')
;
```

… and querying the table you will see the following rows.

```
1    SELECT * FROM sales;
```

	year	month	month_name	date	amount
1	2020	1	JAN	1	10
2	2020	1	JAN	1	15
3	2020	2	FEB	2	20
4	2020	2	FEB	6	60
5	2020	3	MAR	9	90
6	2020	4	APR	9	95
7	2020	5	MAY	10	100
8	2021	2	FEB	4	40
9	2021	2	FEB	5	50
10	2022	2	FEB	6	60

The queries in Example 1.1.A. and 1.1.B. below compares the use of sum function as aggregate function and window function, respectively.

The sum function sum(amount) sums the amounts of the rows with the same year. Each year has its own sum(amount).

The **OVER** clause as in Example 1.1.B indicates that the function is a window function.

Example 1.1.A. sum function used as an aggregate function

```
SELECT year, sum(amount)
FROM sales
GROUP BY year;
```

```
1   SELECT year, sum(amount)
2   FROM sales
3   GROUP BY year;
4
```

year	sum(amount)
1	2020	390
2	2021	90
3	2022	60

Example 1.1.B. sum function used as a window function

```
SELECT year, month, month_name, date, amount,
       sum(amount) OVER(PARTITION BY year ORDER BY date
       ROWS BETWEEN UNBOUNDED PRECEDING AND UNBOUNDED FOLLOWING) sa
FROM sales;
```

```
1   SELECT year, month, month_name, date, amount,
2   sum(amount) OVER(PARTITION BY year ORDER BY date
3   ROWS BETWEEN UNBOUNDED PRECEDING AND UNBOUNDED FOLLOWING) sa
4   FROM sales;
```

	year	month	month_name	date	amount	sa
1	2020	1	JAN	1	10	390
2	2020	1	JAN	1	15	390
3	2020	2	FEB	2	20	390
4	2020	2	FEB	6	60	390
5	2020	3	MAR	9	90	390
6	2020	4	APR	9	95	390
7	2020	5	MAY	10	100	390
8	2021	2	FEB	4	40	90
9	2021	2	FEB	5	50	90
10	2022	2	FEB	6	60	60

While the aggregate function produces **three rows** for the three year, the
window function produces **all rows** from the table. But, their sum(quantity)
are as expected for each of the three years, as can be seen on the last column,
sa.

Window function syntax

So that you know the parts of window function, here is the window function syntax diagram.

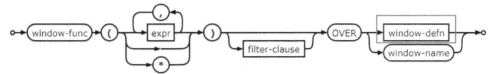

And, the following is window-defn syntax showing its parts.

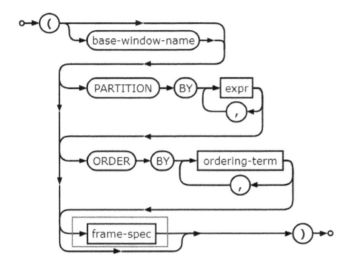

And, next diagram is the frame-spec syntax.

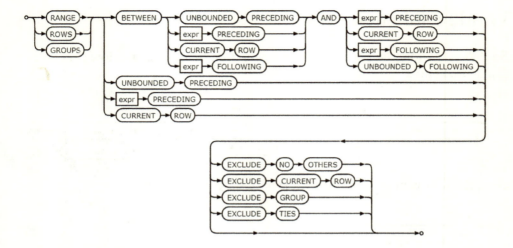

In the next chapters we will delve into each part step-by-step with examples.

Summary

In this chapter you were introduced to window function. You specifically learned that:

- Window function has an OVER clause
- Output of window function is all rows from the table
- The result of window function is a select column

In the next chapter, you will learn the first part of the OVER clause, the PARTITION BY.

Chapter 2 PARTITION BY clause

A partition is a boundary where the aggregation by the window function resets.

As you can see on the syntax diagram below, the PARTITION clause (highlighted by rectangular box)

- is optional
- if it presents must be the first clause, before the ORDER BY clause
- can have one or more expr argument (expression)

Figure 2.1 Window definition syntax

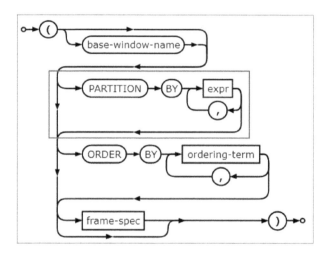

In Example 2.1 below the sum(amount) results is in column sa.

In the example, year is the partition, hence the aggregation column sa resets when the year flips from 2020 to 2021, and then 2021 to 2022. The sa resets to 90 from 390, and then to 60 from 90.

Example 2.1. PARTITION BY year

```
SELECT year, month, month_name, date, amount,
     sum(amount) OVER(PARTITION BY year
```

```
        ORDER BY date
        ROWS BETWEEN UNBOUNDED PRECEDING AND UNBOUNDED FOLLOWING) sa
FROM sales;
```

```
1    SELECT year, month, month_name, date, amount,
2        sum(amount) OVER(PARTITION BY year
3        ORDER BY date
4        ROWS BETWEEN UNBOUNDED PRECEDING AND UNBOUNDED FOLLOWING) sa
5    FROM sales;
6
```

	year	month	month_name	date	amount	sa
1	2020	1	JAN	1	10	390
2	2020	1	JAN	1	15	390
3	2020	2	FEB	2	20	390
4	2020	2	FEB	6	60	390
5	2020	3	MAR	9	90	390
6	2020	4	APR	9	95	390
7	2020	5	MAY	10	100	390
8	2021	2	FEB	4	40	90
9	2021	2	FEB	5	50	90
10	2022	2	FEB	6	60	60

Optional

As can be seen on the syntax diagram Figure 2.1 above, PARTITION BY is optional. If we don't have PARTITION BY, all rows will be treated as one partition as demonstrated in Example 2.2. below. The sum(quantity) is the sum of all rows' quantities, 540.

Example 2.1 No PARTITION BY
```
SELECT year, month, month_name, date, amount,
        sum(amount) OVER(
        ORDER BY date
        ROWS BETWEEN UNBOUNDED PRECEDING AND UNBOUNDED FOLLOWING) sa
FROM sales;
```

```
1    SELECT year, month, month_name, date, amount,
2        sum(amount) OVER(ORDER BY date
3        ROWS BETWEEN UNBOUNDED PRECEDING AND UNBOUNDED FOLLOWING) sa
4    FROM sales;
```

	year	month	month_name	date	amount	sa
1	2020	1	JAN	1	10	540
2	2020	1	JAN	1	15	540
3	2020	2	FEB	2	20	540
4	2021	2	FEB	4	40	540
5	2021	2	FEB	5	50	540
6	2020	2	FEB	6	60	540
7	2022	2	FEB	6	60	540
8	2020	3	MAR	9	90	540
9	2020	4	APR	9	95	540
10	2020	5	MAY	10	100	540

Multiple Expressions

You can put in more than one expression as seen on the syntax diagram above.

In Example 2.3 the PARTITION BY has two expressions: year and month in this order. Notice that now the aggregation column sa resets every time the year and month changes.

Example 2.3 Multiple expressions

```
SELECT year, month, month_name, date, amount,
       sum(amount) OVER(PARTITION BY year, month
       ORDER BY date
       ROWS BETWEEN UNBOUNDED PRECEDING AND UNBOUNDED FOLLOWING) sa
FROM sales;
```

```
1    SELECT year, month, month_name, date, amount,
2      sum(amount) OVER(PARTITION BY year, month
3        ORDER BY date
4        ROWS BETWEEN UNBOUNDED PRECEDING AND UNBOUNDED FOLLOWING) sa
5    FROM sales;
6
```

	year	month	month_name	date	amount	sa
1	2020	1	JAN	1	10	25
2	2020	1	JAN	1	15	25
3	2020	2	FEB	2	20	80
4	2020	2	FEB	6	60	80
5	2020	3	MAR	9	90	90
6	2020	4	APR	9	95	95
7	2020	5	MAY	10	100	100
8	2021	2	FEB	4	40	90
9	2021	2	FEB	5	50	90
10	2022	2	FEB	6	60	60

Computed Expression

In Example 2.4 below the expression is concatenation of date and month_name columns.

Example 2.4 PARTITION BY month_name || year

```
SELECT year, month, date, month_name, amount,
       sum(amount) OVER(PARTITION BY date || month_name, year
       ORDER BY date
       ROWS BETWEEN UNBOUNDED PRECEDING AND UNBOUNDED FOLLOWING) sa
FROM sales;
```

```
1   SELECT year, month, date, month_name, amount,
2      sum(amount) OVER(PARTITION BY date || month_name, year
3      ORDER BY date
4      ROWS BETWEEN UNBOUNDED PRECEDING AND UNBOUNDED FOLLOWING) sa
5   FROM sales;
6
```

	year	month	date	month_name	amount	sa	
1	2020	5	10	MAY	100	100	
2	2020	1	1	JAN	10	25	←
3	2020	1	1	JAN	15	25	
4	2020	2	2	FEB	20	20	←
5	2021	2	4	FEB	40	40	←
6	2021	2	5	FEB	50	50	←
7	2020	2	6	FEB	60	60	←
8	2022	2	6	FEB	60	60	
9	2020	4	9	APR	95	95	←
10	2020	3	9	MAR	90	90	←

Summary

In this chapter you learned that a window function is applied to the rows partition by partition. Further, it can have more than one expression and an expression can be computed, not just a column from the table in the query.

In the next chapter we will move with the other part of the window definition, the ORDER BY clause.

Chapter 3 ORDER BY Clause

The ORDER BY on the OVER clause has the following syntax.

Figure 3.1 ORDER BY syntax

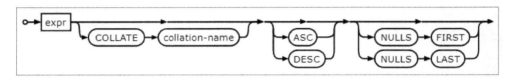

ORDER BY orders the rows **before** applying the computation by the window function. A different order can produce different result.

In Example 3.1.A the order by date is ascending (ASC is the default), while in Example 3.1.B is descending (DESC). The result of Example 3.1.A is different from Example 3.1.B.

Example 3.1.A date ASCENDING (the default)

```
SELECT year, month_name, date, amount,
       sum(amount) OVER(PARTITION BY year
       ORDER BY date ASC
       ROWS BETWEEN UNBOUNDED PRECEDING AND CURRENT ROW) sa
FROM sales;
```

```
1    SELECT year, month_name, date, amount,
2        sum(amount) OVER(PARTITION BY year
3        ORDER BY date
4        ROWS BETWEEN UNBOUNDED PRECEDING AND CURRENT ROW) sa
5    FROM sales;
6
```

	year	month_name	date	amount	sa
1	2020	JAN	1	10	10
2	2020	JAN	1	15	25
3	2020	FEB	2	20	45
4	2020	FEB	6	60	105
5	2020	MAR	9	90	195
6	2020	APR	9	95	290
7	2020	MAY	10	100	390
8	2021	FEB	4	40	40
9	2021	FEB	5	50	90
10	2022	FEB	6	60	60

Example 3.1.B order_date DESC

```
SELECT year, month_name, date, amount,
       sum(amount) OVER(PARTITION BY year
       ORDER BY date ASC
       ROWS BETWEEN UNBOUNDED PRECEDING AND CURRENT ROW) sa
FROM sales;
```

```
1    SELECT year, month_name, date, amount,
2        sum(amount) OVER(PARTITION BY year
3        ORDER BY date DESC
4        ROWS BETWEEN UNBOUNDED PRECEDING AND CURRENT ROW) sa
5    FROM sales;
6
```

	year	month_name	date	amount	sa
1	2020	MAY	10	100	100
2	2020	MAR	9	90	190
3	2020	APR	9	95	285
4	2020	FEB	6	60	345
5	2020	FEB	2	20	365
6	2020	JAN	1	10	375
7	2020	JAN	1	15	390
8	2021	FEB	5	50	50
9	2021	FEB	4	40	90
10	2022	FEB	6	60	60

ORDER BY must be after PARTITION BY

If there's a PARTITION BY, the ORDER BY must be after it; otherwise your query will get into an error.

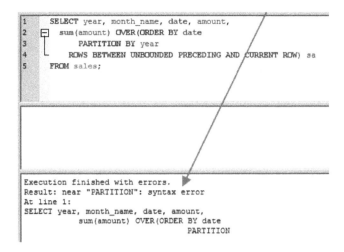

```
1    SELECT year, month_name, date, amount,
2        sum(amount) OVER(ORDER BY date
3            PARTITION BY year
4          ROWS BETWEEN UNBOUNDED PRECEDING AND CURRENT ROW) sa
5    FROM sales;
```

Execution finished with errors.
Result: near "PARTITION": syntax error
At line 1:
SELECT year, month_name, date, amount,
        sum(amount) OVER(ORDER BY date
                                PARTITION

Multiple ordering-term

As you can see on the Figure 3.2 syntax diagram below, we can have more than one ordering term.

Figure 3.2 multiple ordering expressions

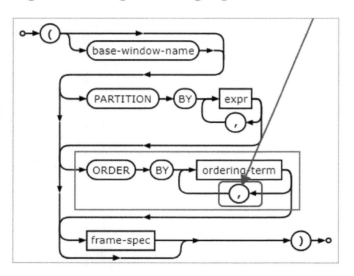

Example 3.2 below has two ORDER BY expressions.

Example 3.2. Two expressions

```
SELECT year, date, month_name, amount,
       sum(amount) OVER(PARTITION BY year
       ORDER BY year DESC, month_name
       ROWS BETWEEN UNBOUNDED PRECEDING AND CURRENT ROW) sa
FROM sales;
```

The following screenshot shows the result.

```
1    SELECT year, date, month_name, amount,
2      sum(amount) OVER(PARTITION BY year
3      ORDER BY year DESC, month_name
4      ROWS BETWEEN UNBOUNDED PRECEDING AND CURRENT ROW) sa
5    FROM sales;
6
7
8
```

	year	date	month_name	amount	sa
1	2020	9	APR	95	95
2	2020	2	FEB	20	115
3	2020	6	FEB	60	175
4	2020	1	JAN	10	185
5	2020	1	JAN	15	200
6	2020	9	MAR	90	290
7	2020	10	MAY	100	390
8	2021	4	FEB	40	40
9	2021	5	FEB	50	90
10	2022	6	FEB	60	60

ORDER BY on the SELECT

The ORDER BY in the OVER clause influences only on the computation by the window function.

If you want to control the ordering of the final output rows apply ORDER BY on the SELECT statement.

In Example 3.3 we order the final output by the sa column

Example 3.3 Ordering final output rows

```
SELECT year, date, month_name, amount,
       sum(amount) OVER(PARTITION BY year
       ORDER BY year DESC, month_name
       ROWS BETWEEN UNBOUNDED PRECEDING AND CURRENT ROW) sa
FROM sales
ORDER BY sa;
```

The following screenshot shows the result.

```
1    SELECT year, date, month_name, amount,
2      sum(amount) OVER(PARTITION BY year
3        ORDER BY year DESC, month_name
4        ROWS BETWEEN UNBOUNDED PRECEDING AND CURRENT ROW) sa
5    FROM sales
6    ORDER BY sa;
7
8
```

	year	date	month_name	amount	sa
1	2021	4	FEB	40	40
2	2022	6	FEB	60	60
3	2021	5	FEB	50	90
4	2020	9	APR	95	95
5	2020	2	FEB	20	115
6	2020	6	FEB	60	175
7	2020	1	JAN	10	185
8	2020	1	JAN	15	200
9	2020	9	MAR	90	290
10	2020	10	MAY	100	390

Chapter 4 Frame Specification

Frame specification is at the heart window function.

While PARTITION BY sets the boundary where aggregating gets reset, frame specification sets the boundary of a current row. Current row is the row being computed for its aggregation value.

In the following syntax diagram the frame spec is in the highlighted box.

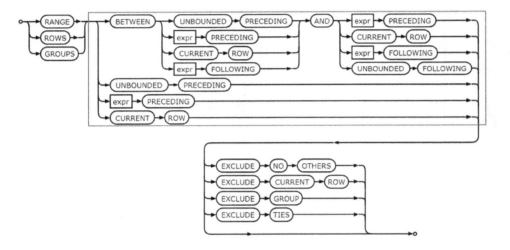

As mentioned above, a current row is the row being computed by the window function. As the window function is computed for every row, every row will be a current row.

A frame for a current window has a start row and end row. These rows are the boundary for the current row. Start row, end row, and all rows between them, unless otherwise specifically excluded, are included in the computation (aggregation) by the window function.

Let's take a look at Example 4.1 below.

Example 4.1 Boundaries of current row number 5.

```
SELECT year, date, amount,
       sum(amount) OVER(PARTITION BY year
       ORDER BY date
       ROWS BETWEEN UNBOUNDED PRECEDING AND CURRENT ROW) sa
FROM sales;
```

Refer to the output in the following figure.

The boundary is specified by BETWEEN UNBOUNDED PRECEEDING AND CURRENT ROW, which, for current row number 5 for example, the row number 1 is the start row and 5 is the end row. The rows included in aggregation calculation are row 1, 2, 3, 4 and 5.

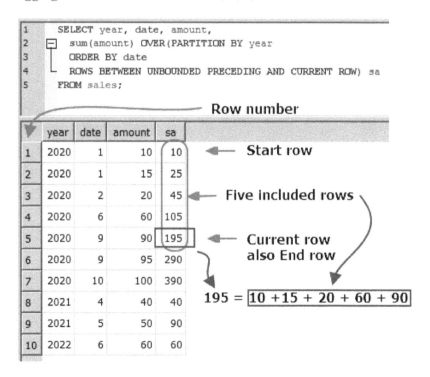

The following figure shows the frame and its sum(quantity) for current row number 1. As row number 1 does not have any preceding row, the start row, current row and end row is the same, row number 1. Hence, its sum(quantity) is only its own quantity 10.

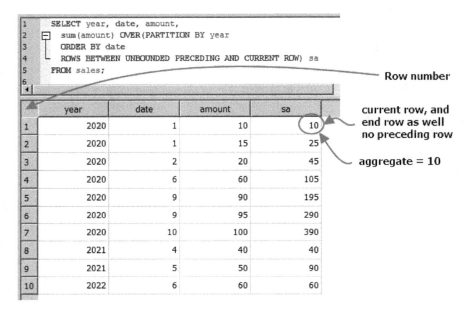

As you can see on the following figure, for row 2 as current row we only have one preceding row, so rows included are two only, row 1 and row 2.

```
1    SELECT year, date, amount,
2  ⊟   sum(amount) OVER(PARTITION BY year
3        ORDER BY date
4  └    ROWS UNBOUNDED PRECEDING AND CURRENT ROW) sa
5      FROM sales;
```

	year	date	amount	sa
1	2020	1	10	10
2	2020	1	15	25
3	2020	2	20	45
4	2020	6	60	105
5	2020	9	90	195
6	2020	9	95	290
7	2020	10	100	390
8	2021	4	40	40
9	2021	5	50	90
10	2022	6	60	60

Only two preceding rows

Current row 2

Aggregation
25 = 10 + 15

The following figure has the frame identification for current row number 9. Row number 9 is in partition 2021, a different partition from the previous two examples, which is partition 2020. Note that partition year 2021 has only two rows, row numbers 8 and 9.

Figure 4.4 frame for curent row 1

```
1    SELECT year, date, amount,
2       sum(amount) OVER(PARTITION BY year
3       ORDER BY date
4       ROWS BETWEEN UNBOUNDED PRECEDING AND CURRENT ROW) sa
5    FROM sales;
6
```

Row number

year	date	amount	sa
1	2020	1	10	10
2	2020	1	15	25
3	2020	2	20	45
4	2020	6	60	105
5	2020	9	90	195
6	2020	9	95	290
7	2020	10	100	390
8	2021	4	40	40
9	2021	5	50	90
10	2022	6	60	60

start row

current row, and end row as well

aggregate 40 + 50

FOLLOWING

So far you learn the use of PRECEDING and CURRENT ROW. Example 4.2 has FOLLOWING.

Example 4.2 FOLLOWING

```
SELECT year, date, amount,
       sum(amount) OVER(PARTITION BY year
       ORDER BY date
       ROWS BETWEEN 1 PRECEDING AND 2 FOLLOWING) sa
FROM sales;
```

In the following figure you can see the included rows for current row 5, and its aggregation.

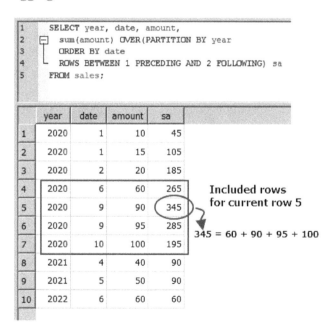

BETWEEN PRECEDING AND PRECEDING

Looks strange, but yes you can set PRECEDING AND PRECEDING or
even FOLLOWING AND FOLLOWING.

Example 4.3 has PRECEDING AND PRECEDING in the frame spec of the
query.

Example 4.3 2 PRECEDING AND 1 PRECEDING

```
SELECT year, date, amount,
       sum(amount) OVER(PARTITION BY year
       ORDER BY date
       ROWS BETWEEN 2 PRECEDING AND 1 PRECEDING) sa
FROM sales;
```

Note that the first preceding's must be greater or the same than the second.

```
1    SELECT year, date, amount,
2        sum(amount) OVER(PARTITION BY year
3        ORDER BY date
4        ROWS BETWEEN 2 PRECEDING AND 1 PRECEDING) sa
5    FROM sales;
```

	year	date	amount	sa	
1	2020	1	10	NULL	
2	2020	1	15	10	
3	2020	2	20	25	◄── included rows
4	2020	6	60	35	
5	2020	9	90	80	◄── current row
6	2020	9	95	150	
7	2020	10	100	185	aggregation 80 = 60 + 20
8	2021	4	40	NULL	
9	2021	5	50	40	
10	2022	6	60	NULL	

BETWEEN FOLLOWING AND FOLLOWING

Example 4.4 has FOLLOWING AND FOLLOWING in the frame spec of the query.

Figure 4.4 2 FOLLOWING AND 1 FOLLOWING

```
SELECT year, date, amount,
       sum(amount) OVER(PARTITION BY year
       ORDER BY date
       ROWS BETWEEN 1 FOLLOWING AND 2 FOLLOWING) sa
FROM sales;
```

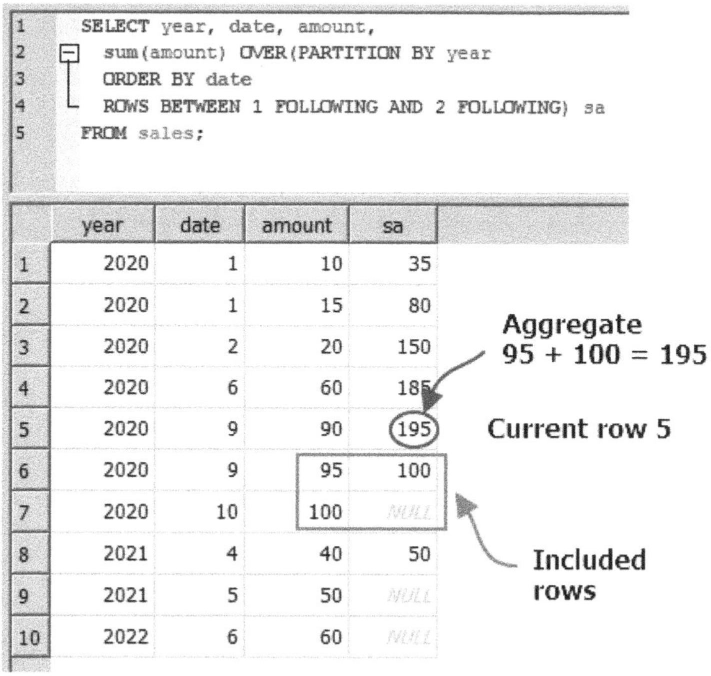

```
1    SELECT year, date, amount,
2        sum(amount) OVER(PARTITION BY year
3        ORDER BY date
4        ROWS BETWEEN 1 FOLLOWING AND 2 FOLLOWING) sa
5    FROM sales;
```

	year	date	amount	sa
1	2020	1	10	35
2	2020	1	15	80
3	2020	2	20	150
4	2020	6	60	185
5	2020	9	90	195
6	2020	9	95	100
7	2020	10	100	NULL
8	2021	4	40	50
9	2021	5	50	NULL
10	2022	6	60	NULL

Aggregate
95 + 100 = 195

Current row 5

Included rows

SIMPLIFIED FRAME

You can also specify a frame boundary without BETWEEN, the options are highlighted in the syntax diagram below.

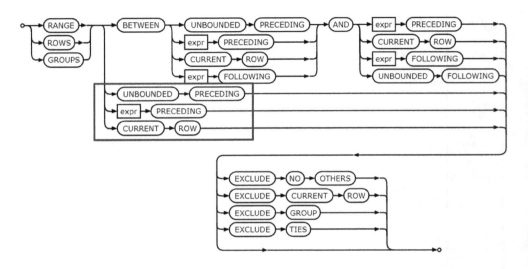

UNBOUNDED PRECEDING

UNBOUNDED PRECEDING is the same as UNBOUNDED
PRECEDING AND CURRENT ROW. We already have this specification in
Example 4.1, reproduced below as Example 4.5.

Example 4.5 UNBOUNDED PRECEDING AND CURRENT ROW

```
SELECT year, date, amount,
       sum(amount) OVER(PARTITION BY year
       ORDER BY date
       ROWS UNBOUNDED PRECEDING) sa
FROM sales;
```

```
1    SELECT year, date, amount,
2  ⊟   sum(amount) OVER(PARTITION BY year
3       ORDER BY date
4    └  ROWS UNBOUNDED PRECEDING) sa
5    FROM sales;
```

	year	date	amount	sa
1	2020	1	10	10
2	2020	1	15	25
3	2020	2	20	45
4	2020	6	60	105
5	2020	9	90	195
6	2020	9	95	290
7	2020	10	100	390
8	2021	4	40	40
9	2021	5	50	90
10	2022	6	60	60

expr PRECEDING

expr PRECEDING is the same as expr PRECEDING AND CURRENT ROW.

Example 4.6 2 PRECEDING

```
SELECT year, date, amount,
       sum(amount) OVER(PARTITION BY year
       ORDER BY date
       ROWS 2 PRECEDING) sa
FROM sales;
```

```
1   SELECT year, date, amount,
2     sum(amount) OVER(PARTITION BY year
3     ORDER BY date
4     ROWS 2 PRECEDING) sa
5   FROM sales;
```

	year	date	amount	sa
1	2020	1	10	10
2	2020	1	15	25
3	2020	2	20	45
4	2020	6	60	95
5	2020	9	90	170
6	2020	9	95	245
7	2020	10	100	285
8	2021	4	40	40
9	2021	5	50	90
10	2022	6	60	60

Included two rows

current row 2

Aggregate
25 = 10 + 15

CURRENT ROW

CURRENT ROW means only the current row is included in the aggregation, which is not that useful.

Example 4.7 uses CURRENT ROW

```
SELECT year, date, amount,
       sum(amount) OVER(PARTITION BY year
       ORDER BY date
       ROWS CURRENT ROW) sa
FROM sales;
```

```
1    SELECT year, date, amount,
2       sum(amount) OVER(PARTITION BY year
3       ORDER BY date
4       ROWS CURRENT ROW) sa
5    FROM sales;
```

	year	date	amount	sa
1	2020	1	10	10
2	2020	1	15	15
3	2020	2	20	20
4	2020	6	60	60
5	2020	9	90	90
6	2020	9	95	95
7	2020	10	100	100
8	2021	4	40	40
9	2021	5	50	50
10	2022	6	60	60

FRAME TYPES

Window function requires a frame type. Frame types can be ROWS, RANGE, or GROUPS, as shown on the syntax.

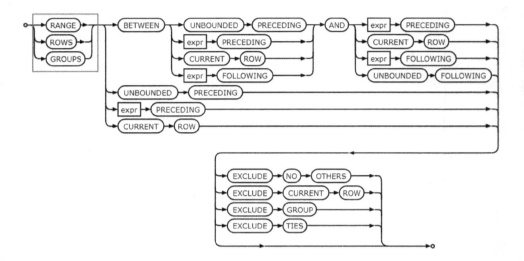

Frame type influences the boundaries.

While row of ROWS refers to the **row number,** row of RANGE refers to the expr value of the ORDER BY.

Example 4.8 and its output in the following figure illustrate the differences among the three frame types.

The annotation in the figure is for current row number 6.

ROWS refers to the row number. In the example, the boundary 2 PRECEDING AND CURRENT ROW means row numbers 4, 5, and 6 are rows to be included in the sum(amount) computation. Hence, the result of sum(amount) for current row 6 is $(90 + 60 + 100) = 250$.

RANGE refers to the expr of the ORDER BY. In the example, with expr **month** in the ORDER BY, the boundary 2 PRECEDING AND CURRENT ROW means the rows with month = 4 and 5 before the current row and current row (month = 5 as well) are the expected rows to be included in the sum(amount) computation. But, the month 5 is not available. So, we have three rows included: one row with month 3 and two rows with month 5. Hence, the result of sum(amount) for current row 6 is (60 + 100 + 100) = 260.

GROUPS also refers to the expr of the ORDER BY. But, instead of the value of expr, it refers to **whatever row(s) available within the boundary and rows with the same expr value are included.** In the example, with expr month in the ORDER BY, the boundary 2 PRECEDING AND CURRENT ROW means the rows with month = 2 and 3 before the current row and current row 6 (month = 5 as well) are the expected rows to be included in the sum(amount) computation. So, we have six rows included: three rows with month 2, one row with month = 3, and two rows with month 5. Hence, the result of sum(amount) is (20 + 20 + 90 + 60 + 100 + 100) = 390.

Example 4.8 ROWS, RANGE and GROUPS

```
SELECT year,
row_number() OVER(PARTITION BY year ORDER BY month) "row number",
amount,
sum(amount) OVER(PARTITION BY year ORDER BY month ROWS 2 PRECEDING)
rw,
row_number() OVER(PARTITION BY year ORDER BY month) "row number",
month, amount,
sum(amount) OVER(PARTITION BY year ORDER BY month RANGE 2
PRECEDING) ra,
row_number() OVER(PARTITION BY year ORDER BY month) "row number",
month, amount,
sum(amount) OVER(PARTITION BY year ORDER BY month GROUPS 2
PRECEDING) gr
FROM sales;
```

```
1   select year,
2   row_number() OVER(PARTITION BY year ORDER BY month) "row number",
3   amount,
4   sum(amount) OVER(PARTITION BY year ORDER BY month ROWS 2 PRECEDING) rw,
5   row_number() OVER(PARTITION BY year ORDER BY month) "row number",
6   month, amount,
7   sum(amount) OVER(PARTITION BY year ORDER BY month RANGE 2 PRECEDING) ra,
8   row_number() OVER(PARTITION BY year ORDER BY month) "row number",
9   month, amount,
10  sum(amount) OVER(PARTITION BY year ORDER BY month GROUPS 2 PRECEDING) gr
11  FROM sales;
```

three rows for ROWS type sum(amount) = 250

three rows for RANGE type sum(amount) = 260

three rows for GROUPS type sum(amount) = 390

CURRENT ROW

	year	row number	amount	rw	row number	month	amount	ra	row number	month	amount	gr
1	2020	1	10	10	1	1	10	10	1	1	10	10
2	2020	2	20	30	2	2	20	140	2	2	20	140
3	2020	3	20	50	3	2	20	140	3	2	20	140
4	2020	4	90	130	4	2	90	140	4	2	90	140
5	2020	5	60	170	5	3	60	200	5	3	60	200
6	2020	6	100	250	6	5	100	260	6	5	100	390
7	2020	7	100	260	7	5	100	260	7	5	100	390
8	2021	1	50	50	1	2	50	50	1	2	50	50
9	2021	2	50	100	2	3	50	100	2	3	50	100
10	2022	1	60	60	1	2	60	60	1	2	60	60

FILTER

In this section you will learn the filter-clause that you can specify. Filter-clause is optional part of window function. It must be right before the OVER, as shown in the window-function syntax diagram below. Note that filter-clause is **optional**.

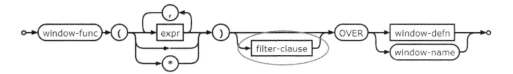

Here is the syntax of the filter-clause.

o→(FILTER)→((→(WHERE)→expr→())→o

Rows in the frame that do not satisfy the expr of the WHERE are **excluded from the computation** by the window function. The rows that do not satisfy are still on the output, only they are not included in the computation.

Example 4.9 FILTER

```
SELECT year, amount,
       sum(amount)
       FILTER (WHERE year = 2020) -- only 2020 is computed
            OVER(PARTITION BY year ORDER BY (amount) DESC
            ROWS BETWEEN UNBOUNDED PRECEDING AND CURRENT ROW) saf
FROM sales;
```

```
1   SELECT year, amount,
2     sum(amount)
3     FILTER (WHERE year = 2020) -- only 2020 is computed
4       OVER(PARTITION BY year ORDER BY (amount) DESC
5       ROWS BETWEEN UNBOUNDED PRECEDING AND CURRENT ROW) saf
6   FROM sales;
```

	year	amount	saf	
1	2020	100	100	
2	2020	100	200	
3	2020	100	300	
4	2020	60	360	
5	2020	20	380	
6	2020	20	400	
7	2020	10	410	
8	2021	50	NULL	**Excluded from**
9	2021	50	NULL	**computing the**
10	2022	60	NULL	**sum(amount)**

EXCLUDE

While FILTER specifies only the rows in the frame to be included in the aggregation, EXCLUDE specifies those to be excluded. EXCLUDE is **optional**.

Below syntax diagram shows the position of EXLUDE within the frame spec and its options.

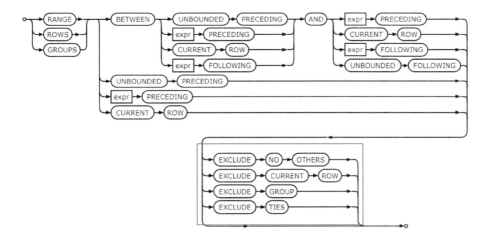

Here are the meaning of the options:
- **EXCLUDE NO OTHERS**: No row in the frame is excluded.
- **EXCLUDE CURRENT ROW**: Current row is excluded. Peer rows remain for the GROUPS and RANGE frame types.
- **EXCLUDE GROUP**: Current row and its peer rows are excluded.
- **EXCLUDE TIES**: Peer rows of the current row are excluded.

EXCLUDE is optional. The default (if not specified) is EXCLUDE NO OTHERS.

Example 4.10 demonstrates that EXCLUDE NO OTHERS for all three frame types produce the same result as without EXCLUDE clause.

Example 4.10 EXCLUDE NO OTHERS

```
SELECT year, month,
row_number() OVER(PARTITION BY year ORDER BY month) rn, amount,
sum(amount) OVER(PARTITION BY year ORDER BY month ROWS 2 PRECEDING)
RW,
sum(amount) OVER(PARTITION BY year ORDER BY month ROWS 2 PRECEDING
EXCLUDE NO OTHERS) RWeno, sum(amount) OVER(PARTITION BY year ORDER
BY month RANGE 2 PRECEDING
EXCLUDE NO OTHERS) RAeno, sum(amount) OVER(PARTITION BY year ORDER
BY month GROUPS 2 PRECEDING
EXCLUDE NO OTHERS) GReno
FROM sales;
```

```
1    SELECT year, month,
2    row_number() OVER(PARTITION BY year ORDER BY month) rn, -- row number
3    amount,
4    sum(amount) OVER(PARTITION BY year ORDER BY month ROWS 2 PRECEDING) RW, -- no EXCLUDE
5    sum(amount) OVER(PARTITION BY year ORDER BY month ROWS 2 PRECEDING
6    EXCLUDE NO OTHERS) RWeno, -- no row is excluded, hence sum(amount) is the same as previous column rn
7    sum(amount) OVER(PARTITION BY year ORDER BY month RANGE 2 PRECEDING
8    EXCLUDE NO OTHERS) RAeno, -- no row is excluded, hence sum(amount) is the same as previous column rn
9    sum(amount) OVER(PARTITION BY year ORDER BY month GROUPS 2 PRECEDING
10   EXCLUDE NO OTHERS) GReno -- no row is excluded, hence sum(amount) is the same as previous column rn
11   FROM sales;
```

	year	month	rn	amount	RW	RWeno	RAeno	GReno
1	2020	1	1	10	10	10	10	10
2	2020	2	2	20	30	30	140	140
3	2020	2	3	20	50	50	140	140
4	2020	2	4	90	130	130	140	140
5	2020	3	5	60	170	170	200	200
6	2020	5	6	100	250	250	260	390
7	2020	5	7	100	260	260	260	390
8	2021	2	1	50	50	50	50	50
9	2021	3	2	50	100	100	100	100
10	2022	2	1	60	60	60	60	60

EXCLUDE CURRENT ROW is in Example 4.11. For current row number 6 its output is annotated with explanation on the impact of this clause for the three frame types.

Example 4.11 EXCLUDE CURRENT ROW

```
SELECT year, month, amount,
```

```
sum(amount) OVER(PARTITION BY year ORDER BY month ROWS 2 PRECEDING
EXCLUDE CURRENT ROW) RWcrr, -- ROWS type current row is excluded
month, amount,
sum(amount) OVER(PARTITION BY year ORDER BY month RANGE 2 PRECEDING
EXCLUDE CURRENT ROW) RAcrr, -- RANGE type current row is excluded
month, amount,
sum(amount) OVER(PARTITION BY year ORDER BY month GROUPS 2
PRECEDING
EXCLUDE CURRENT ROW) GRcrr -- GROUPS type current row is excluded
FROM sales;
```

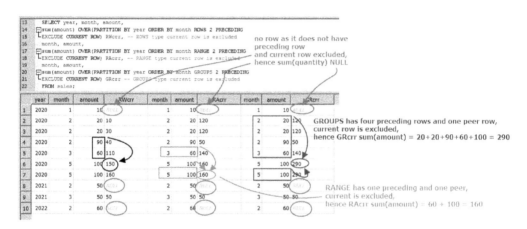

EXCLUDE GROUP is in Example 4.12. For current row number 6 its output is annotated with explanation on the impact of this clause for the three frame types.

Example 4.12 EXCLUDE GROUP

```
SELECT year, month, amount,
sum(amount) OVER(PARTITION BY year ORDER BY month ROWS 2 PRECEDING
EXCLUDE GROUP) RWeg, -- ROWS type current row and ite peers are
excluded
month, amount,
sum(amount) OVER(PARTITION BY year ORDER BY month RANGE 2 PRECEDING
EXCLUDE GROUP) RAeg, -- RANGE type current row and ite peers are
excluded
month, amount,
sum(amount) OVER(PARTITION BY year ORDER BY month GROUPS 2
PRECEDING
EXCLUDE GROUP) GReg -- GROUPS type current row and ite peers are
excluded
FROM sales;
```

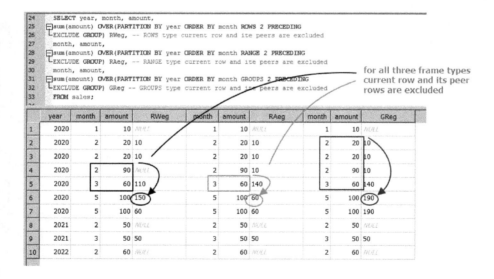

EXCLUDE TIES is in Example 4.13. For current row number 6 its output is annotated with explanation on the impact of this clause for the three frame types.

Example 4.13 EXCLUDE TIES

```
SELECT year, month, amount,
sum(amount) OVER(PARTITION BY year ORDER BY month ROWS 2 PRECEDING
EXCLUDE CURRENT ROW) RWcrr, -- ROWS type peers of the current row
are excluded
month, amount,
sum(amount) OVER(PARTITION BY year ORDER BY month RANGE 2 PRECEDING
EXCLUDE CURRENT ROW) RAcrr, -- RANGE type peers of the current row
are excluded
month, amount,
sum(amount) OVER(PARTITION BY year ORDER BY month GROUPS 2
PRECEDING
EXCLUDE CURRENT ROW) GRcrr -- GROUPS type peers of the current row
are excluded
FROM sales;
```

	year	month	amount	RWcrr	month	amount	RAcrr	month	amount	GRcrr
1	2020	1	10		1	10		1	10	
2	2020	2	20	10	2	20	120	2	20	120
3	2020	2	20	30	2	20	120	2	20	120
4	2020	2	90	40	2	90	50	2	90	50
5	2020	3	60	110	3	60	140	3	60	140
6	2020	5	100	150	5	100	160	5	100	290
7	2020	5	100	160	5	100	160	5	100	290
8	2021	2	50		2	50		2	50	
9	2021	3	50	50	3	50	50	3	50	50
10	2022	2	60		2	60		2	60	

current row is included, but its peers are excluded

Chapter 5 Aggregate Window Functions

The sum function we used in previous examples is one of the aggregate window functions provided in SQLite.

Here is the list and descriptions of aggregate window functions:
- sum(X)
- total(X)
- avg(X)
- count(X)
- count(*)
- max(X)
- min(X)
- group_concat(X,Y)

In this chapter, you will learn every one of these functions. Every function is defined, example and output of example query is shown and annotated as necessary to explain.

sum(X) and total(X)

In the previous examples you already used sum(X). Below you will learn more, and in particular its difference from the total function.

sum(X) and total(X) return the sum of numeric X of included rows (rows in the frame of current row). While sum does not include NULL, total does. If all X is NULL, sum returns NULL, total returns 0.0.

Example 5.1 sum and total

```
SELECT year, month, amount,
       sum(amount) OVER(PARTITION BY year
             ORDER BY (year||month) DESC ROWS BETWEEN UNBOUNDED
PRECEDING AND CURRENT ROW) sq, -- sum quantity
       typeof(
             sum(amount) OVER(PARTITION BY year
```

```
                ORDER BY (year||month) DESC ROWS BETWEEN UNBOUNDED
PRECEDING AND CURRENT ROW)) sqt, -- type of sum
        total(amount) OVER (PARTITION BY year
                ORDER BY year||month DESC ROWS BETWEEN UNBOUNDED
PRECEDING AND CURRENT ROW) tq, -- total quantity
        typeof(
                total(amount) OVER (PARTITION BY year
                ORDER BY year||month DESC ROWS BETWEEN UNBOUNDED
PRECEDING AND CURRENT ROW)) tqt -- type of total
FROM sales;
```

```sql
1    SELECT year, month, amount,
2    sum(amount) OVER(PARTITION BY year
3        ORDER BY (year||month) DESC ROWS BETWEEN UNBOUNDED PRECEDING AND CURRENT ROW) sq, -- sum quantity
4    typeof(
5        sum(amount) OVER(PARTITION BY year
6        ORDER BY (year||month) DESC ROWS BETWEEN UNBOUNDED PRECEDING AND CURRENT ROW)) sqt, -- type of sum
7    total(amount) OVER (PARTITION BY year
8        ORDER BY year||month DESC ROWS BETWEEN UNBOUNDED PRECEDING AND CURRENT ROW) tq, -- total quantity
9    typeof(
10       total(amount) OVER (PARTITION BY year
11       ORDER BY year||month DESC ROWS BETWEEN UNBOUNDED PRECEDING AND CURRENT ROW)) tqt -- type of total
12   FROM sales;
13
```

	year	month	amount	sq	sqt	tq	tqt	
1	2020	5	100	100	integer	100.0	real	
2	2020	5	100	200	integer	200.0	real	
3	2020	3	100	300	integer	300.0	real	non integer/real
4	2020	2	20.5	320.5	real	320.5	real	
5	2020	2	60.5	381.0	real	381.0	real	
6	2020	1	9	390.0	real	390.0	real	NULL
7	2021	3	NULL	NULL	null	0.0	real	
8	2021	2	50	50	integer	50.0	real	
9	2021	2	50	100	integer	100.0	real	
10	2022	2	60	60	integer	60.0	real	

AVG(X)

avg(X) returns the average value of X. The result of avg() is always a real number (floating point value). The result is NULL if all X are NULL.

Example 5.2 avg

```
SELECT year, month, amount,
       avg(amount) OVER(PARTITION BY year
             ORDER BY (year||month) DESC ROWS BETWEEN UNBOUNDED
PRECEDING AND CURRENT ROW) aq, -- average quantity
       typeof(
             avg(amount) OVER(PARTITION BY year
             ORDER BY (year||month) DESC ROWS BETWEEN UNBOUNDED
PRECEDING AND CURRENT ROW)) taq -- type of average
FROM sales;
```

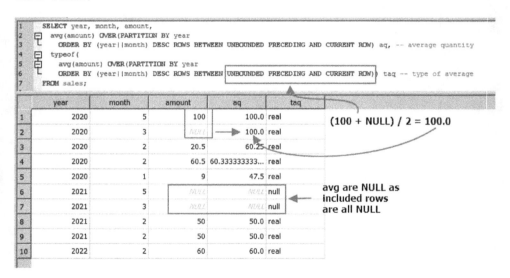

COUNT(X) and COUNT(*)

count(*) returns the total number of rows including NULL, while COUNT(X) does not include NULL.

Example 5.3 count

```
SELECT year, month, amount,
       count(*)  OVER(PARTITION BY year
                  ORDER BY (year||month) DESC ROWS BETWEEN UNBOUNDED
PRECEDING AND CURRENT ROW) cnt, -- count
       count(amount) OVER(PARTITION BY year
                  ORDER BY (year||month) DESC ROWS BETWEEN UNBOUNDED
PRECEDING AND CURRENT ROW) cntq -- count quantity
FROM sales;
```

```
1    SELECT year, month, amount,
2      count(*) OVER(PARTITION BY year
3        ORDER BY (year||month) DESC ROWS BETWEEN UNBOUNDED PRECEDING AND CURRENT ROW) cnt, -- count
4      count(amount) OVER(PARTITION BY year
5        ORDER BY (year||month) DESC ROWS BETWEEN UNBOUNDED PRECEDING AND CURRENT ROW) cntq -- count quantity
6    FROM sales;
7
```

	year	month	amount	cnt	cntq
1	2020	5	100	1	1
2	2020	3	NULL	2	1
3	2020	2	20.5	3	2
4	2020	2	60.5	4	3
5	2020	1	9	5	4
6	2021	5	NULL	1	0
7	2021	3	NULL	2	0
8	2021	2	50	3	1
9	2021	2	50	4	2
10	2022	2	60	1	1

max(X) and min(X)

max(X) and min(X) return the maximum value and minimum amount of X. The maximum value is the value that would be returned last in an ORDER BY on the same column; the minimum, first. If all X are NULL, the functions return NULL.

Example 5.4 max and min

```
SELECT year, month, amount,
       max(amount) OVER(PARTITION BY year
              ORDER BY (year||month) DESC ROWS BETWEEN UNBOUNDED
PRECEDING AND CURRENT ROW) ma, -- maximum
       min(amount) OVER(PARTITION BY year
              ORDER BY (year||month) DESC ROWS BETWEEN UNBOUNDED
PRECEDING AND CURRENT ROW) mi -- minimum
FROM sales;
```

```
1    SELECT year, month, amount,
2      max(amount) OVER(PARTITION BY year
3        ORDER BY (year||month) DESC ROWS BETWEEN UNBOUNDED PRECEDING AND CURRENT ROW) ma, -- maximum
4      min(amount) OVER(PARTITION BY year
5        ORDER BY (year||month) DESC ROWS BETWEEN UNBOUNDED PRECEDING AND CURRENT ROW) mi -- minimum
6    FROM sales;
7
```

	year	month	amount	ma	mi
1	2020	5	100	100	100
2	2020	3	NULL	100	100
3	2020	2	20.5	100	20.5
4	2020	2	60.5	100	20.5
5	2020	1	9	100	9
6	2021	5	NULL	NULL	NULL
7	2021	3	NULL	NULL	NULL
8	2021	2	50	50	50
9	2021	2	50	50	50
10	2022	2	60	60	60

group_concat(X, Y)

group_concat(X,Y) returns a string which is the concatenation of all non-NULL values of X. Y is used as the separator between each of X. A comma (,) is used as the separator if Y is omitted.

Example 5.5 group_concat

```
SELECT year, month_name,
       group_concat(month_name, ' | ') OVER(PARTITION BY year -- |
separator
               ORDER BY (year||month) DESC ROWS BETWEEN UNBOUNDED
PRECEDING AND CURRENT ROW) gc -- group concat
FROM sales;
```

```
1    SELECT year, month_name,
2      group_concat(month_name, ' | ') OVER(PARTITION BY year -- | separator
3        ORDER BY (year||month) DESC ROWS BETWEEN UNBOUNDED PRECEDING AND CURRENT ROW) gc -- group concat
4    FROM sales;
5
```

	year	month_name	gc
1	2020	MAY	MAY
2	2020	NULL	MAY
3	2020	FEB	MAY | FEB
4	2020	FEB	MAY | FEB | FEB
5	2020	JAN	MAY | FEB | FEB | JAN
6	2021	MAY	MAY
7	2021	FEB	MAY | FEB
8	2021	FEB	MAY | FEB | FEB
9	2021	NULL	MAY | FEB | FEB
10	2022	FEB	FEB

Chapter 6 Built-in Window function

The so called **built-in window** functions are not aggregating. Below is the list of all built-in window functions.

Here is the list of the built-in window functions.
- row_number
- rank
- dense_rank
- percent_rank
- cume_dist
- ntile
- lag
- lead
- first_value
- last_value
- nth_value

In this chapter, you will learn every one of the above functions. Every function is defined, example and output of example query is shown and annotated as necessary to further explain.

row_number()

row_number function finds the number of the row within the current partition. Rows are numbered starting from 1 in the order defined by the ORDER BY clause in the window definition, or in arbitrary order otherwise.

row_number() function ignores frame specification.

In Example 6.1 **rnA** is computed without frame specification, while **rnB** has a frame specification. They produce the same result.

Example 6.1 row_number without and with frame spec

```
SELECT year, amount,
       row_number() OVER(PARTITION BY year
       ORDER BY amount DESC) rnA,
             row_number() OVER (PARTITION BY year
               ORDER BY amount DESC ROWS BETWEEN 2 FOLLOWING AND
UNBOUNDED FOLLOWING) rnB
FROM sales;
```

```
1    SELECT year, amount,
2      row_number() OVER(PARTITION BY year
3      ORDER BY amount DESC) rnA,
4        row_number() OVER (PARTITION BY year
5        ORDER BY amount DESC ROWS BETWEEN 2 FOLLOWING AND UNBOUNDED FOLLOWING) rnB
6    FROM sales;
```

	year	amount	rnA	rnB
1	2020	100	1	1
2	2020	100	2	2
3	2020	90	3	3
4	2020	60	4	4
5	2020	20	5	5
6	2020	15	6	6
7	2020	10	7	7
8	2021	50	1	1
9	2021	40	2	2
10	2022	60	1	1

rank() and dense_rank()

rank() function returns the row_number() of each group of peer rows starting from 1 in the order as specified by ORDER BY clause.

dense_rank() also returns rank number similar to rank().

The difference between rank() and dense_rank() is that while rank() has gap if a peer group has more than one row, dense_rank() does not have gap.

With rank(), the next rank number jumps as many as the number of gaps. Figure 6.2 shows 2 gaps and 1 gap.

Similar to row_number() function, frame specification is also ignored.

Example 6.2 rank() and dense_rank()

```
SELECT year, amount,
   rank() OVER (PARTITION BY year ORDER BY amount DESC) rnk,
   dense_rank() OVER (PARTITION BY year ORDER BY amount DESC) drnk
FROM sales;
```

If there's no ORDER BY then all rows are considered peers and this function always returns rank 1 as demonstrated in Example 6.3.

```
1   SELECT year, amount,
2   rank() OVER (PARTITION BY year) rnk,
3   dense_rank() OVER (PARTITION BY year ) drnk
4   FROM sales;
```

	year	amount	rnk	drnk
1	2020	10	1	1
2	2020	20	1	1
3	2020	20	1	1
4	2020	60	1	1
5	2020	100	1	1
6	2020	100	1	1
7	2020	100	1	1
8	2021	50	1	1
9	2021	50	1	1
10	2022	60	1	1

percent_rank()

percent_rank() returns a value between 0.0 and 1.0 equal to **(rank - 1)/(partition-rows - 1)**, where **rank** is the value returned by built-in window function rank() and **partition-rows** is the total number of rows in the partition.

If the partition contains **only one row**, this function returns **0.0**.

Example 6.3 shows the percent_rank calculation.

```
SELECT year, amount,
   rank() OVER (PARTITION BY year ORDER BY amount) rnk,
   percent_rank() OVER (PARTITION BY year ORDER BY amount) prnk
FROM sales;
```

Example 6.3 calculation of percent_rank()

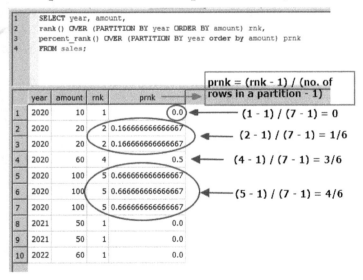

cume_dist()

cume_dist() returns the cumulative distribution. Calculated as *row-number/partition-rows*, where *row-number* is the value returned by row_number() for the last peer in the group and *partition-rows* the number of rows in the partition.

Example 6.4 shows the cume_dist calculation for the rows in partition year 2020.

Example 6.4 cume_dist()

```
SELECT year, amount,
       row_number() OVER(PARTITION BY year ORDER BY (amount) ) rn,
       cume_dist() OVER(PARTITION BY year ORDER BY (amount) ) cd
FROM sales;
```

ntile(N)

ntile(N) divides a partition into N groups, where the number of rows distributed in the N groups are as evenly as possible. Then, ntile(N) returns an integer between 1 and N to each group, in the order defined by the ORDER BY clause, or in arbitrary order otherwise. If necessary, larger groups occur first.

In Example 6.5 N is 3.

Example 6.5 ntile(3)

```
SELECT year, amount,
   ntile(3) OVER (PARTITION BY year ORDER BY amount) ntile3
FROM sales;
```

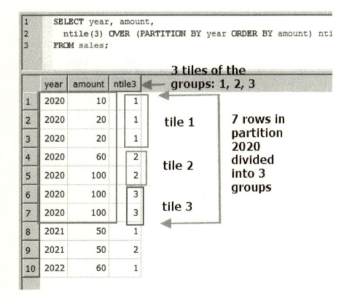

lag and lead

lag(expr, offset, default) and **lead(expr, offset, default)** return the result of evaluating expression **expr** against the previous row and the next row in the partition, respectively.

If there is no previous or next row because the current row is the first or last row, then the functions return NULL.

If the *offset* argument is provided, then it must be a non-negative integer. In this case the value returned is the result of evaluating *expr* against the row *offset* rows before or after the current row within the partition.

If *offset* is 0, then *expr* is evaluated against the current row. If there is no row *offset* rows before the current row, NULL is returned.

If *default* is also provided, then it is returned instead of NULL if the row identified by *offset* does not exist.

In Example 6.6 below both lag and lead have offset 1 and default 'NA'

Example 6.6 lag and lead

```
SELECT year, month, amount,
lag((amount), 1, 'NA') OVER (PARTITION BY year ORDER BY amount) lg,
lead((amount), 1, 'NA') OVER (PARTITION BY year ORDER BY amount) ld
FROM sales;
```

```
1   SELECT year, amount,
2     lag((amount), 1, 'NA') OVER (PARTITION BY year ORDER BY amount) lg,
3     lead((amount), 1, 'NA') OVER (PARTITION BY year ORDER BY amount) ld
4   FROM sales;
```

	year	amount	lg	ld
1	2020	10	NA	20	lag 1 before is none, default to NA; lead 1 after is 20
2	2020	20	10	20	lag 1 before is 10; lead 1 after is 20
3	2020	20	20	60	lag 1 before is 20; lead 1 after is 60
4	2020	60	20	100	lag 1 before is 20; lead 1 after is 100
5	2020	100	60	100
6	2020	100	100	100
7	2020	100	100	NA
8	2021	50	NA	50
9	2021	50	50	NA
10	2022	60	NA	NA

first_value, last_value and nth_value

These three functions require window frame for each row

first_value(expr) and last_value(expr) return the value of **expr** evaluated against the first and last row, respectively, in the window frame, for each row. If there is no first or last row then they return NULL.

nth_value(expr, N) in the same way as an aggregate window function, and returns the value of **expr** evaluated against the row N of the window frame. If there is no Nth row in the partition, then NULL is returned.

Example 6.6 first_value and last_value

```
SELECT year, amount,
       first_value(amount) OVER(PARTITION BY year
       ORDER BY amount DESC      ROWS BETWEEN 2 FOLLOWING AND
UNBOUNDED FOLLOWING) fv,
       last_value(amount) OVER(PARTITION BY year
       ORDER BY amount DESC      ROWS BETWEEN 2 FOLLOWING AND
UNBOUNDED FOLLOWING) lv,
       nth_value(amount,2) OVER(PARTITION BY year
       ORDER BY amount DESC      ROWS BETWEEN 2 FOLLOWING AND
UNBOUNDED FOLLOWING) nv
FROM sales;
```

```
1    SELECT year, amount,
2
3      first_value(amount) OVER(PARTITION BY year
4      ORDER BY amount DESC  ROWS BETWEEN 2 FOLLOWING AND UNBOUNDED FOLLOWING) fv,
5      last_value(amount) OVER(PARTITION BY year
6      ORDER BY amount DESC  ROWS BETWEEN 2 FOLLOWING AND UNBOUNDED FOLLOWING) lv,
7      nth_value(amount,2) OVER(PARTITION BY year
8      ORDER BY amount DESC  ROWS BETWEEN 2 FOLLOWING AND UNBOUNDED FOLLOWING) nv
9    FROM sales;
```

nth_value(amount, 2) is
second next row after

	year	amount	fv	lv	nv
1	2020	100	100	10	60
2	2020	100	60	10	20
3	2020	100	20	10	20
4	2020	60	20	10	10
5	2020	20	10	10	NULL
6	2020	20	NULL	NULL	NULL
7	2020	10	NULL	NULL	NULL
8	2021	50	NULL	NULL	NULL
9	2021	50	NULL	NULL	NULL
10	2022	60	NULL	NULL	NULL

Appendix A: Introducing DB Browser for SQLite

The purpose of this appendix is to show you how to use DB Browser for SQLite. It is brief, enough only so you can try the book examples.

Creating table and maintaining data

Start your DB Browser for SQLite from Windows Start menu.

The initial window should look like the following.

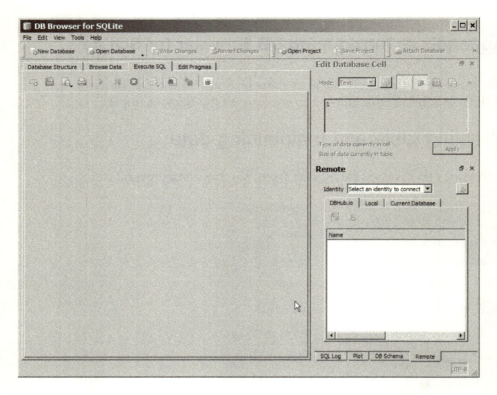

Let's create a database for the book examples by clicking the New Database button.

Determine the folder where you want to store the database file. Name the file for example book.sqlite, and click the Save button.

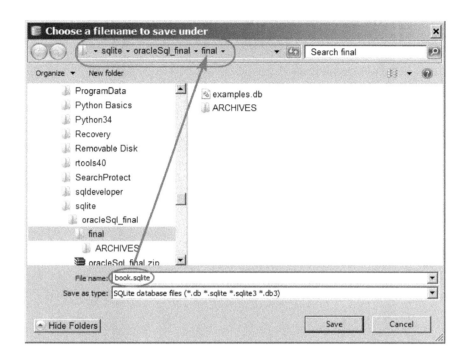

If you get the following Edit table definition window, close it by clicking the Cancel button.

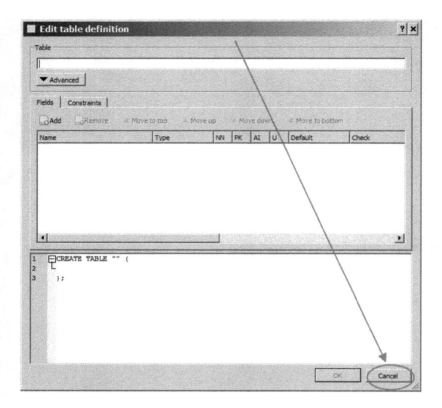

You will be back to the main window.

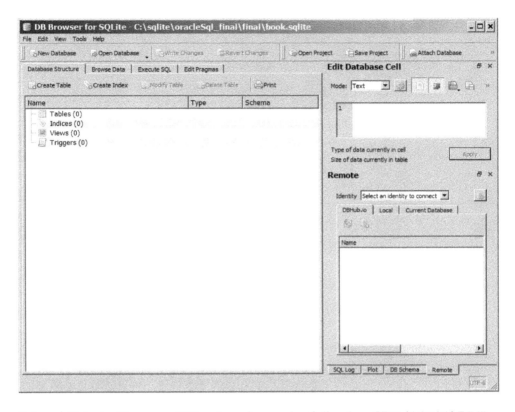

Select/click the Execute SQL tab and type the following CREATE TABLE statement, then press F5 to execute the statement. A message will show up indicating that the statement is successfully executed, the sales table is created in the book.sqlite database.

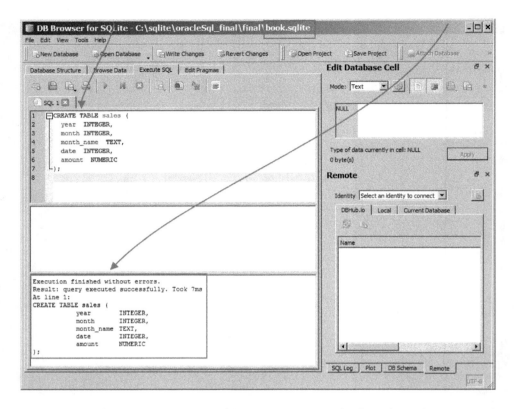

You can confirm that the sales table now exists on the Database Structure tab.

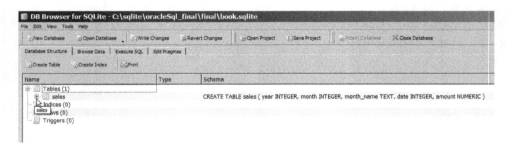

The sales table is still empty. Now, type the following INSERT statement and press Shift + F5 keys to add ten rows into the sales table.

File   Edit   View   Tools   Help

New Database   Open Database   Write Changes   Revert Changes   Open Proj

Database Structure | Browse Data | Execute SQL | Edit Pragmas

SQL 1

```sql
1   CREATE TABLE sales (
2       year   INTEGER,
3       month INTEGER,
4       month_name   TEXT,
5       date  INTEGER,
6       amount   NUMERIC
7   );
8
9   INSERT INTO sales (year, month, month_name, date, amount)
10  VALUES ('2020', '1', 'JAN', '1', '10')
11  ,('2020', '1', 'JAN', '1', '15')
12  ,('2020', '2', 'FEB', '2', '20')
13  ,('2020', '2', 'FEB', '6', '60')
14  ,('2020', '3', 'MAR', '9', '90')
15  ,('2020', '4', 'APR', '9', '95')
16  ,('2020', '5', 'MAY', '10', '100')
17  ,('2021', '2', 'FEB', '4', '40')
18  ,('2021', '2', 'FEB', '5', '50')
19  ,('2022', '2', 'FEB', '6', '60')
20  ;
21
```

```
Execution finished without errors.
Result: query executed successfully. Took 30ms, 10 rows affected
At line 9:
INSERT INTO sales (year, month, month_name, date, amount)
VALUES ('2020', '1', 'JAN', '1', '10')
,('2020', '1', 'JAN', '1', '15')
,('2020', '2', 'FEB', '2', '20')
,('2020', '2', 'FEB', '6', '60')
,('2020', '3', 'MAR', '9', '90')
,('2020', '4', 'APR', '9', '95')
,('2020', '5', 'MAY', '10', '100')
,('2021', '2', 'FEB', '4', '40')
,('2021', '2', 'FEB', '5', '50')
,('2022', '2', 'FEB', '6', '60')
;
```

Query the tables to confirm all ten rows now are in the sales table. Type the select statement and press Shif + F5. The result is on the pane below the editor pane, it should show all ten rows.

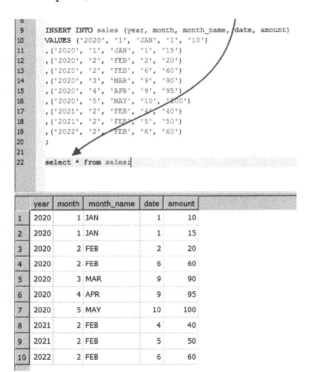

Some of the book examples need different rows. You can edit the data by opening the Browse data tab: update a cell, add a new row, delete existing rows, save the changes, and various other data editing functions. Confirm the changes by pressing the Write Changes button on the top bar.

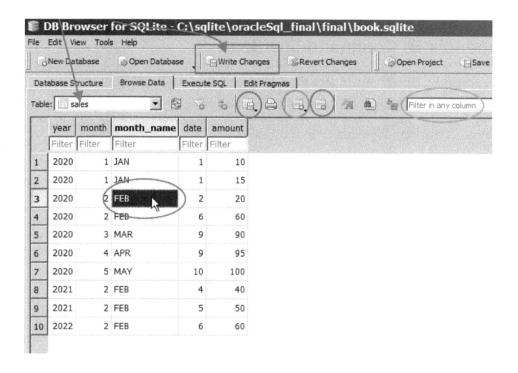

Summary

You now know how to create table, maintain data, and query data in DB Browser for SQLite.

Appendix B: Command-line Shell

This appendix briefly introduces the Command-line shell tool that you can download from https://www.sqlite.org/index.html

Download the item highlighted in red below.

See screenshot below.

Start the Command-line shell from Windows command. Change to the folder where you want to store the database. Then enter sqlite3.

The Command-line shell is ready for your SQL activities, e.g. creating a database. You can enter SQL at the sqlite3> prompt, execute it by pressing Enter. The screenshot shows that you can create table, inserting data, and querying the data. If you make a mistake, you get an error description.

www.ingramcontent.com/pod-product-compliance
Lightning Source LLC
LaVergne TN
LVHW041219050326
832903LV00021B/702